The Trip

Rosanne Keller

New Readers Press
Publishing Division of Laubach Literacy International
Syracuse, New York

ISBN 0-88336-997-4

© 1990
New Readers Press
Publishing Division of
Laubach Literacy International
Box 131, Syracuse, New York 13210

All rights reserved. No part of this book may be reproduced or transmitted in any form or by any means, electronic or mechanical, including photocopying, recording, or by any information storage and retrieval system, without permission in writing from the publisher.

Printed in the United States of America

Edited by Kay Koschnick
Illustrated by Joe Orsak
Cover design by Chris Steenwerth
Cover illustration by Joe Orsak

9 8 7 6 5 4 3 2 1

Table of Contents

1. The Tickets 5
2. Getting to the Bus 9
3. "Las" Something 14
4. The Floor Show 20
5. Trouble 26
6. Da Fu to the Rescue 30

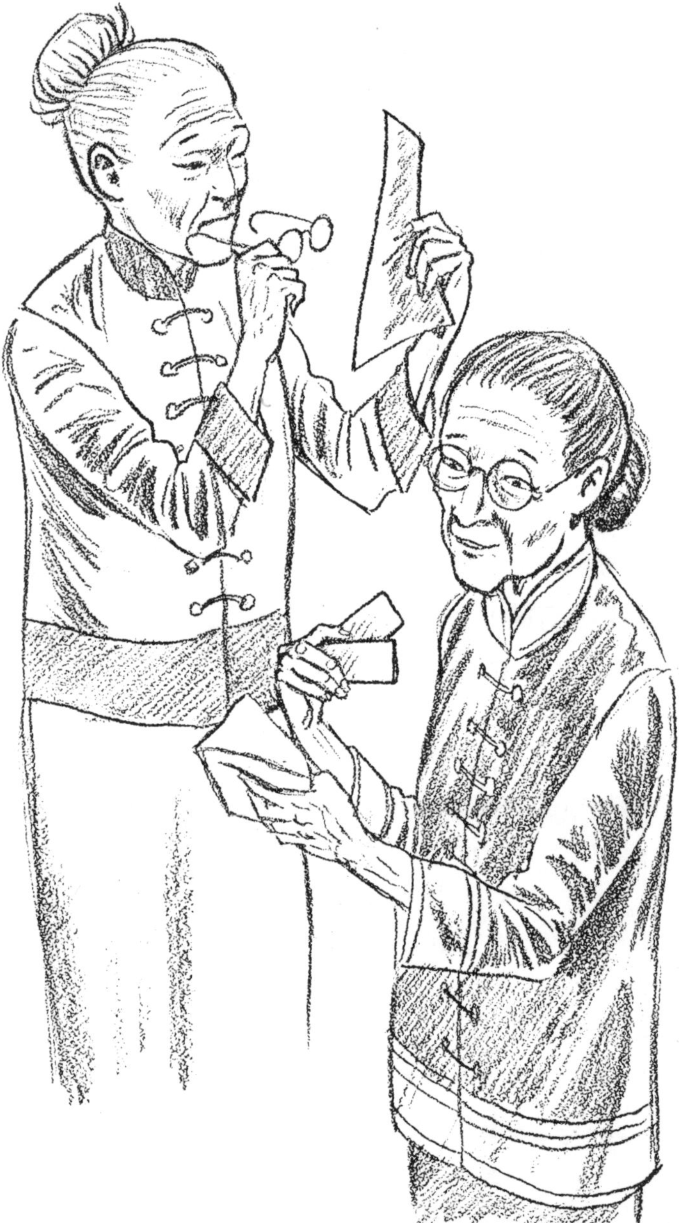

1

The Tickets

Lu Li puts on her glasses. She takes the letter to the window. She rips open the envelope and holds the paper up to the light. "Ah," she says.

"Who is it from?" asks her sister, Lu Shan.

"It's from Da Fu, Elder Sister." Lu Li smiles. She picks up the envelope and looks inside. Then her eyes get big. "O-o-oh!" she says. She pulls out two squares of cardboard. "Look!" she says. She looks at them as if she can read them.

"Younger Sister! Give the letter to me before I feed you to a dragon," Lu Shan says. Lu Li hands the letter to her. It is written in Da Fu's neat Chinese characters.

Da Fu is their nephew. He has lived in America for 10 years.

* * *

Four years ago, Da Fu helped his aunts leave China and come to the U.S. He came to the San Francisco airport to meet them. He brought them to his apartment in Chinatown. After that, they lived with him.

But last year, Da Fu moved to Los Angeles. Now, he works in a famous Chinese restaurant there. He sends them money every week.

The day he left was a sad day for the old ladies. They sat on the sofa for a long time and talked. Lu Li hung onto her sister's hand. "I am 71, and you are 74. We are old. What will we do?" Her voice shook. "And Da Fu. He will have no one to take care of him."

"We will keep a home for Da Fu here," Lu Shan said. "Maybe one day he will come back to San Francisco."

* * *

Now, Lu Shan and Lu Li love getting letters from their nephew. They are excited when one comes today.

Lu Li gives the letter to her older sister. Lu Shan puts on her glasses to read it. Then she looks up at her younger sister. "What is that in your hand?" Lu Shan asks.

"Bus tickets, Elder Sister. Da Fu wants us to come visit him," Lu Li says. "He sent us tickets for the bus. He says to come next Saturday." Lu Li looks at Lu Shan. "Do you think we can?"

Lu Shan reads the letter. Then she answers, "I don't see why not. He tells us just what to do. We take a taxi to the bus station. He says that the bus is an express. That means it doesn't stop. It goes straight to Los Angeles. He will be waiting for us."

"But, Elder Sister," Lu Li says. "We don't speak English. What if we get lost?"

"This is no time to whine, Younger Sister." Lu Shan gives her sister a hard look. "After all, we got to San Francisco from China, didn't we? Surely, we can travel from city to city here."

"I guess so." Lu Li is wringing her hands. "But we have never even been out of Chinatown!"

"Hush," Lu Shan says. "Let's go pack our suitcase. It will be an adventure. We are going out to see the world!"

2

Getting to the Bus

At last, Saturday comes. The sisters wear their best dresses. The dresses have high collars and buttons made of cloth. The dresses were made by a tailor in China many years ago.

Lu Li has on a big straw hat. She bought it for the trip. "I have heard that the sun is very hot in Los Angeles," she explains.

But it is cool in San Francisco. Before they leave, the sisters put on heavy sweaters.

Lu Shan takes the bus tickets. "I'll take the tickets," she says. "Younger Sister, you carry the suitcase."

The sisters go to Mr. Chen's grocery store. Mr. Chen is a friend of theirs. He speaks English. They ask him to call a taxi for them. It comes right away.

Mr. Chen helps them into the taxi. The driver puts their suitcase in the trunk. "I'll tell him where to take you," Mr. Chen says.

The taxi driver takes them to a big building. "The bus to Los Angeles must be in there," Lu Shan says.

The bus station is huge. It is crowded with people. And such noise! There are many doors. The sisters can see buses outside some of the doors.

A man is mopping the floor. "Ask him where to go," Lu Li says. She steps behind Lu Shan.

Lu Shan takes out the tickets. She shows them to the man. He smiles and points to the ticket. Then he points to the other side of the building.

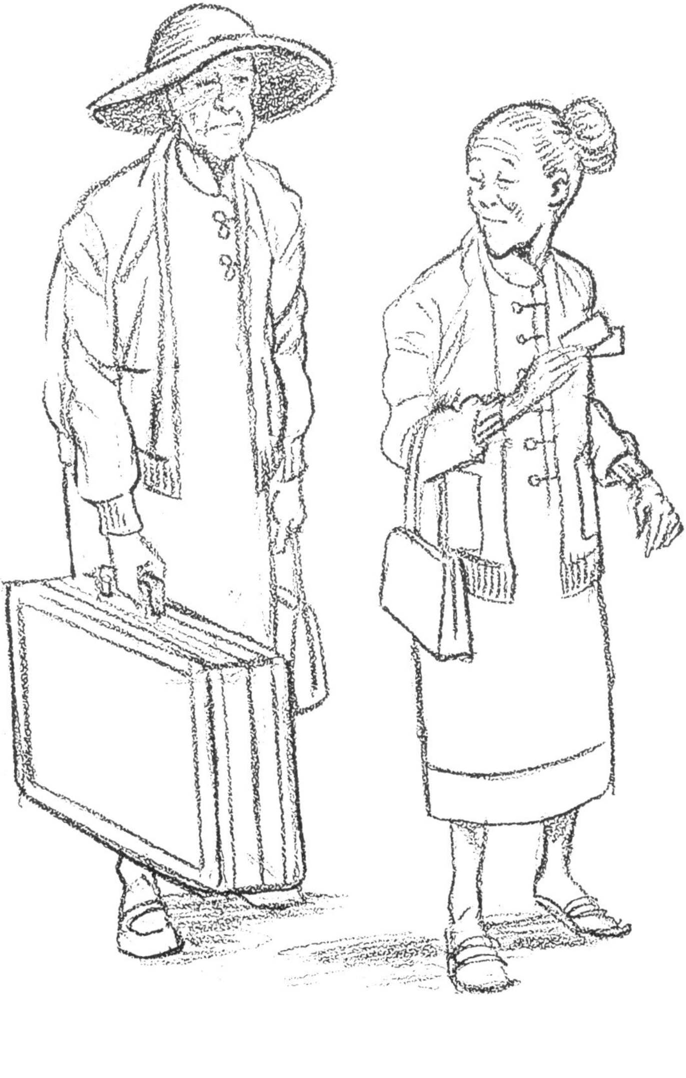

Lu Shan looks at the word under the man's finger—*Los*. Then she sees the sign above a door. It says *Las—Something*. "That is our gate," Lu Shan tells her sister.

The bus driver takes their suitcase and puts it in the side of the bus. Then he helps them up the steps.

Everyone on the bus is happy. They are laughing and talking. Then the driver comes through to pick up everyone's tickets. He seems to be joking with the people. When he talks, they laugh. He doesn't even look at the sisters' tickets.

"Everyone is very cheerful," Lu Li says. She begins to relax. "At least, we don't have to worry now. This bus goes straight to Los Angeles. And Da Fu will be there waiting."

3

"Las" Something

The trip seems long. But finally, the bus stops. "We must be in Los Angeles," Lu Shan says. She looks out the window. "Is this a bus station? How beautiful it is! Da Fu must be inside."

But when they go in, their nephew is not there. Lu Shan and Lu Li sit down in big comfortable chairs. "It's not like Da Fu to be late," Lu Li says. She takes off her hat.

"Don't worry," says Lu Shan. "Maybe he got delayed." Then she notices a young man behind the counter. She sees the people standing in line. They are getting keys. "Younger Sister," Lu Shan says. "This is not a bus station. It's a hotel."

"A hotel?"

"Yes," says Lu Shan. "I understand. Da Fu asked that the bus bring us to this hotel—in case he was late. And now we can wait for him in these soft chairs. Such a nice boy!"

"I hope he won't be too long," Lu Li says. She is looking across the great, shiny floor. "My, this is a grand place." Then she smiles. "Look, there is our suitcase. That man has brought it in for us." She gets up and brings it over.

They sit for a while. Then Lu Shan says, "I think I'll look around."

"But what if Da Fu comes for us?" Lu Li asks.

"He will look for us," Lu Shan answers. "We won't leave the hotel. I want to see what is in there." She points to a wide door with bright lights around it. "Let's go."

Lu Li puts on her hat and picks up the suitcase. They walk through the hotel

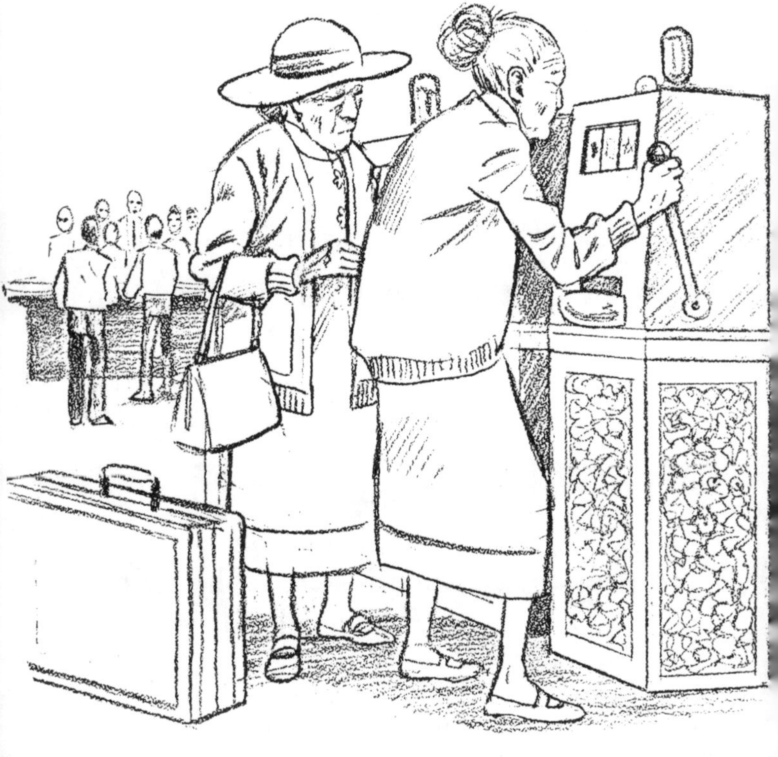

lobby. They go through the door into a huge room. And such a room! There are tables where people are playing cards. There are machines. People are putting in money and pulling on a handle.

"This is a gambling place!" Lu Li says. "Is it all right for us to be here?"

"I'm sure that it is," Lu Shan says. "There are other women here. And everyone is having a good time." They watch the people playing the machines. Sometimes, a few coins come out.

Lu Shan goes up to one machine. A sign on it says *25¢*. She looks at the man beside her at the next machine. She watches where he puts his coin.

"No!" Lu Li says. "Don't!"

"Hush," says Lu Shan. She puts a quarter in the machine. She pulls the handle. Something in the machine turns quickly and stops. Nothing happens. She puts in another quarter and pulls.

Suddenly, a bell starts ringing. A light starts flashing. Money comes pouring out of the machine.

"You broke it!" Lu Li cries. She holds her hands to her cheeks. "We are going to get into trouble. O-o-oh!"

Lu Shan looks around. People are clapping and smiling. They motion for the sisters to pick up the money.

"They are saying to pick it up!" Lu Shan says. She laughs. "Put some in your purse!" Lu Shan picks up handfuls of quarters. She fills her purse with them.

Lu Li looks troubled. "What if the machine is broken?" she asks. "Other people got only a few coins."

"It's all right," Lu Shan says. "Take the money. It's ours! We won it!"

When they turn to leave, they can hardly lift their purses. They go back into the hotel lobby.

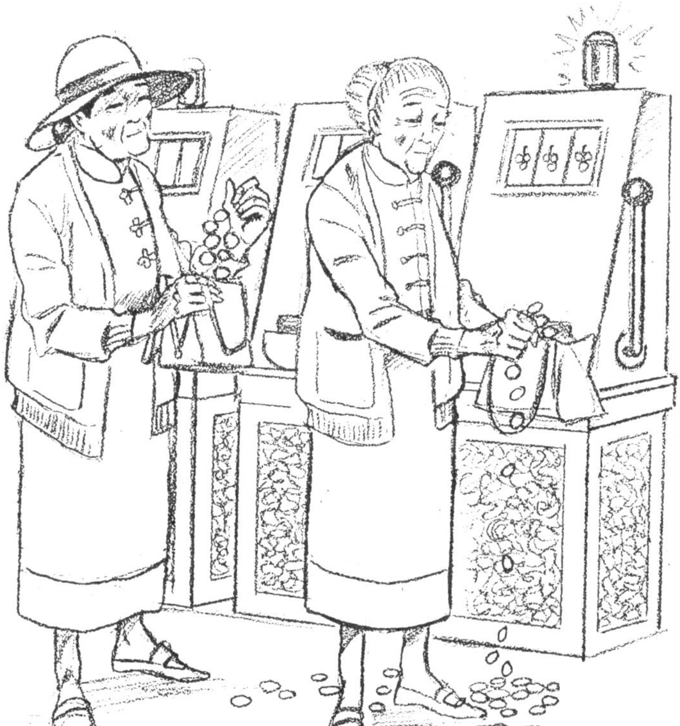

4

The Floor Show

"That made me hungry," Lu Li says. She staggers with her heavy purse in one hand and the suitcase in the other. She looks around the hotel lobby. "Oh, where is Da Fu?" she cries.

"Don't worry so much, Younger Sister," Lu Shan says. "He will come for us. Let's go to that restaurant over there. It's dinnertime, and we have to eat. Da Fu will understand. He will find us. Maybe he will come in time to eat with us."

A man in a black suit stands in the door of the restaurant. He bows to the sisters as they walk in. Someone else takes them to a table.

"Aren't these people nice?" Lu Li giggles. "They treat us like queens."

The waitress brings menus. The sisters look at them. "Elder Sister, do you understand any of this?" Lu Li asks.

Lu Shan turns the pages. She shakes her head.

"We can't read it," Lu Li says. "What will we do?"

"I know," says Lu Shan. "Just point your finger." She shows Lu Li how. "Point to two or three things."

Lu Li carefully chooses things from one page of the menu. Lu Shan chooses things from three different pages.

The waitress shrugs her shoulders and writes on a pad. When she brings the food, Lu Li gasps.

Lu Shan covers her mouth with her hand. She doesn't want to laugh in front of the waitress.

Lu Li gets three desserts: pie, cake, and pudding.

Lu Shan gets a steak dinner. She gets a fish dinner. And she gets a cold drink. The drink has a little paper umbrella standing in it.

Between the two of them, the sisters have a good meal. The drink is wonderful.

After a while, the waitress comes back to the table. She asks a question. But the sisters don't understand. Lu Li points to Lu Shan's drink. Then she points to herself. The waitress brings her a drink, too. It also has a little umbrella.

Suddenly, it gets very dark in the room. A band starts to play. On a stage at the front of the room, bright lights come on. Then a group of girls comes onto the stage. They are dancing. They can kick very high. Lu Shan and Lu Li watch.

Then Lu Shan drops her fork. "One of those girls is taking off her clothes!" she says.

Lu Shan and Lu Li stop eating. "Maybe she can't see all these people," Lu Li says. "Maybe those bright lights are shining in her eyes." She puts her hands to her face. "O-o-oh!"

They can't help watching. Then Lu Li leans forward. "I don't think she has *anything* on now." She looks closer. "No! Just paint—and feathers."

"Well, she must be cold," Lu Shan says. "I think it's chilly in here, don't you?" She takes a sip of her drink. She picks up her fork. "At least, the girls are pretty. If I took off *my* clothes—"

"Lu Shan!" Lu Li whispers. "What a thing to say!" Then they both start laughing. They can't stop.

The waitress brings the check. That makes them stop laughing. The total is $38.50.

"O-o-oh!" Lu Li says. "We have to pay! I thought that Da Fu—"

"Of course, we have to pay," Lu Shan says.

"But we don't have thirty-eight dollars," says Lu Li.

"What about all these quarters we got?" Lu Shan opens her purse.

"Oh," says Lu Li. "Can we spend those?"

Lu Shan just smiles. Giggling, they pile quarters on the table. "Here she comes," Lu Shan whispers.

The waitress looks at the table. She just shakes her head and says something to herself. Then she starts counting the money. People at the other tables are laughing.

"Such nice people!" Lu Li says. The sisters get up to leave. Their purses are still heavy.

5

Trouble

Lu Shan and Lu Li walk toward the restaurant door. "Maybe we can come here again with Da Fu," Lu Li says. "He will like that show."

"Younger Sister!" Lu Shan says. "Da Fu is just a boy!"

"Well, the food is good," Lu Li says. She is trying to hang onto the suitcase and her purse. "He likes a good meal." Her hat falls over one eye. "I wonder why he is so late."

As they come out into the hotel lobby, they hear a shout. Lu Shan stops. "I wonder what is happening," she says. Just then, a man runs up to her.

It is the young man who works behind the counter. He is talking very fast to them. Then he shouts across the room at someone else. He takes Lu Shan's elbow. He hurries across the room with her.

Lu Li runs along behind, dragging the suitcase. "O-o-oh!" she cries. Other people are shouting and pointing. Some men standing nearby turn to watch.

"What has happened?" Lu Shan asks. They don't understand her.

Lu Li grabs her sister's hand. She is shaking. "O-o-oh, where is Da Fu?" Her voice is shaking, too.

"Lu Shan? Lu Li?" The sisters turn to see who is saying their names. It is a policeman!

"O-o-oh!" Lu Li says. "The police! I knew it!"

"He even knows our names," Lu Shan whispers.

"It was wrong to take that money!" says Lu Li. "That machine *was* broken."

27

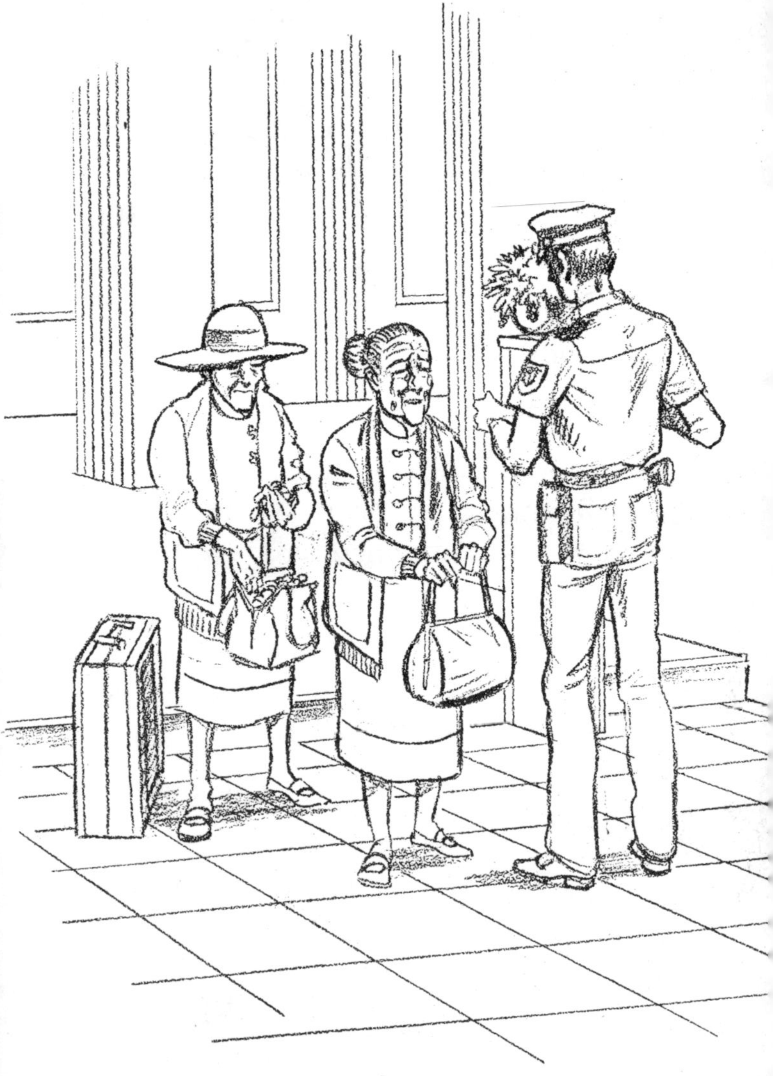

Quickly, she opens her purse and takes out handfuls of quarters. She tries to give them to the policeman.

"Take the money back!" Lu Li says. "We didn't mean to steal." She begins to cry.

The policeman shakes his head and smiles. Then he says, "Da Fu—" The sisters can't understand the rest of his words.

"Oh, no!" says Lu Shan. "Something has happened to Da Fu!" Now *her* voice shakes. Tears roll down her cheeks.

6

Da Fu to the Rescue

The policeman takes Lu Shan's arm. He leads her to the counter. He smiles, shaking his head. He gives her the phone.

"Auntie? Are you there? This is Da Fu." Lu Shan's knees become weak.

"Da Fu! Where are you?" she shouts. "We are worried about you. And now the police are here. They think we stole money! But we didn't! It came out of a machine."

Lu Li grabs the phone. "Da Fu! We are in such trouble!"

"Auntie, listen to me," Da Fu says. "You are not in trouble. You are in Las Vegas."

"Las—not Los Angeles?" Lu Li looks around the hotel. "Where is Las Veg—what?"

"Las Vegas, Nevada," her nephew explains. "You took the wrong bus. I went to meet you at the bus station. But you weren't there. Then I called San Francisco. I talked with Mr. Chen. He said that you took a taxi to the bus station. That is when I called the police."

"The police! Why?"

"To look for you. The police found out that you got on that bus to Las Vegas. The bus is called the Gamblers' Special." Da Fu is laughing. "It's a party bus. People go on that bus to Las Vegas for one night. They go there to see the shows and gamble. Las Vegas is a gambling town."

"Yes, we know," says Lu Li. She puts her heavy purse on the floor and sits down on the suitcase.

"What is he saying?" Lu Shan asks.

"He says we are in Nevada."

Lu Shan takes the phone. "Where is Nevada?" she asks.

"It's a long way from Los Angeles," says Da Fu. "But everything will be all right, Auntie. The police will take you to the bus station. They will put you on a bus to Los Angeles. You will be here before morning."

"Will you be there?" Lu Shan asks.

"Of course," says Da Fu. He laughs. "The policeman said that you hit the jackpot. I want to help you spend all the money that you won!"